Practise Your Phonics With
Julia Donaldson's
Songbirds

OXFORD
UNIVERSITY PRESS

OXFORD
UNIVERSITY PRESS

Great Clarendon Street, Oxford, OX2 6DP, United Kingdom

Oxford University Press is a department of the University of Oxford.
It furthers the University's objective of excellence in research, scholarship
and education by publishing worldwide. Oxford is a registered trade mark
of Oxford University Press in the UK and in certain other countries

Text © Julia Donaldson 2007
Ron Rabbit's Big Day illustrations © Jonathan Allen 2007
The Wishing Elf illustrations © Anni Axworthy 2007
Bob Bug and the Insect Club illustrations © Deborah Allwright 2007
Where is the Snail? illustrations © Kay Widdowson 2007
Stop Chatting, Bill illustrations © Ross Collins 2007
Back to Bed illustrations © Joelle Dreidemy 2007

The moral rights of the author have been asserted

First Edition published 2007
This Edition published 2012

British Library Cataloguing in Publication Data
Data available

978-0-19-279300-3

10 9

Printed in China

Paper used in the production of this book is a natural, recyclable product
made from wood grown in sustainable forests. The manufacturing process
conforms to the environmental regulations of the country of origin.

Acknowledgements
Series editor Clare Kirtley

Helping your child's learning
with free eBooks, essential
tips and fun activities
www.oxfordowl.co.uk

Songbirds

Ron Rabbit's Big Day

Story by Julia Donaldson
Pictures by Jonathan Allen
Series editor Clare Kirtley

OXFORD
UNIVERSITY PRESS

3

Tips for reading Ron Rabbit's Big Day together

This book practises this letter pattern:

ee

Ask your child to point to this letter pattern and say the sound (*ee* as in *need*). Look out for this letter pattern in the story.

Your child might find these words tricky:

of to the no he one two new bottle for have they after are was she says all her about Mr Mrs

These words are common, but your child may not be able to sound them out yet. Say the words for your child if they do not know them.

Before you begin, ask your child to read the title by sounding out and blending as much as possible. Look at the picture together. What do you think the story is about?

Remind your child to read unfamiliar words by saying the individual sounds separately and then blending them together quickly to read the word. When you have finished reading the story, look through it again and:

- Ask your child, *Why did Ron trip the man up?* (He was stealing things from Mr Preston.)

- Point to the letter pattern that makes the long vowel sound in *creeping*. Say what sound this letter pattern makes (*ee*). Find and read some more words in the book which contain the letter pattern *ee* (*needs, three, need, sees, green, asleep*).

Ron Rabbit has a new job. He is a milkman.

Ron has to get up at six. The sun is not up yet.

Ron fills his van with milk. Then he sets off.

clink clink

Mrs Jessop needs one bottle of milk. Ron dumps it on the step.

Two bottles for Miss Quin. Three bottles for Mr Chang.

Mr and Mrs Preston have ten children. They need ten bottles of milk!

Ron is getting the bottles from his van when he sees a man. The man is creeping along.

Is it Mr Preston? No, this man is not as thin, and he has a big black sack on his back.

When the man sees Ron he runs. "Stop!" yells Ron. He runs after the man.

Ron trips the man up. The man drops the sack and Ron grabs it. The man runs off.

In the sack are lots of things … a clock, a pink jug, a big cup, a green lamp, and a cash box!

cash box

Ron rings the bell. Mrs Preston is cross. "I was asleep, Ron," she says.

But then she sees all the things, and Ron tells her about the bad man. "Thank you, Ron!" says Mrs Preston.

Mr Preston rings the cops.

The cops catch the bad man.

Ron gets a medal.

Songbirds
The Wishing Elf

Story by Julia Donaldson
Pictures by Anni Axworthy
Series editor Clare Kirtley

OXFORD
UNIVERSITY PRESS

Tips for reading The Wishing Elf together

This book practises this letter pattern:

ie

Ask your child to point to this letter pattern and say the sound (*ie* as in *tie*). Look out for this letter pattern in the story.

Your child might find these words tricky:

I   to   the   of   come   school   he   you   all
one   says   was   for   everyone   now   have
another   your   what   do

These words are common, but your child may not be able to sound them out yet. Say the words for your child if they do not know them.

Before you begin, ask your child to read the title. Remind your child to read words they do not recognise by sounding out and blending. Look at the picture together. What do you think this story is about?

Remind your child to read unfamiliar words by saying the individual sounds separately and then blending them together quickly to read the word. When you have finished reading the story, look through it again and:

- Ask your child, *Why did Miss Smith wish for an extra hand?* (She had lots of things to do.)

- Find and read two words on page 31 which rhyme (*tries, flies*). Point to the letter pattern that makes the long vowel sound in these words. Say what sound this letter pattern makes (*ie*). Point to the beginning two letters in each word. Say each sound they make. Think of other words which begin with the two sounds *fl* or *tr* (e.g. *flag, flap, fly, trip, trap, tree*).

An elf has come to school! He is standing on Miss Smith's desk. "You can all have one wish," he says.

"I wish I had a parrot," says Dan.

The elf claps his hands. "Abracadabra!" he says. The next second, a parrot flies in!

"I wish I was rich," says Kevin.

"I wish I had wings," says Yasmin.

Meg wishes for a big pie and lots of chips.

Majid wishes for a forest!

"I wish I had a dragon," says Gwen.

A dragon flies in. It tries to get the parrot. Miss Smith has to tie it up.

"I wish I sat next to Patrick," says Ross.

But then Patrick says, "I wish I sat next to Callum."

Everyone gets a wish.

"Now Miss Smith must have a wish," says the elf. Miss Smith thinks. "I wish I had an extra hand!" she says.

The next second, Miss Smith has an extra hand. "Now I can do lots of things," she says.

"I must visit another school now," says the elf.

If the elf visits your school, what will you wish for?

Songbirds

Bob Bug and the Insect Club

Story by Julia Donaldson

Pictures by Deborah Allwright

Series editor Clare Kirtley

OXFORD
UNIVERSITY PRESS

Tips for reading Bob Bug and the Insect Club together

This book practises this letter pattern:

oa

Ask your child to point to this letter pattern and say the sound (*oa* as in *toad*). Look out for this letter pattern in the story.

Your child might find these words tricky:

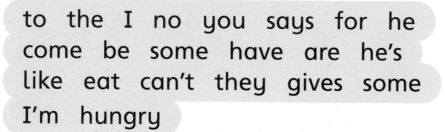

to   the   I   no   you   says   for   he   come   be   some   have   are   he's   like   eat   can't   they   gives   some   I'm   hungry

These words are common, but your child may not be able to sound them out yet. Say the words for your child if they do not know them.

Before you begin, ask your child to read the title. Remind your child to read words they do not recognise by sounding out and blending. Look at the picture together. What do you think this story is about?

Remind your child to read unfamiliar words by saying the individual sounds separately and then blending them together quickly to read the word. When you have finished reading the story, look through it again and:

- Ask your child, *Why wasn't Bob hungry?* (He had eaten toast, nuts and buns in his Club for Insects.)

- Point to the letter pattern that makes the long vowel sound in *cockroach*. Say what sound this letter pattern makes (*oa*). Find and read some more words in the book which contain the letter pattern *oa* (*toast, toad, toads, roast*).

Bob Bug and his mum are in the kitchen. Bob has a pen and a pad.

"Can you spell 'insects'?" says Bob.
"Yes," says Mum.

Bob sticks this on his den:
"Club for Insects".

Bob is sitting in his den. Ant taps on the den. "I am an insect," he says. "Can I come in?"

"Yes," says Bob. "You can be in the club."

Ant brings some toast. "Thank you," says Bob. Ant and Bob sit in the den and munch the toast.

Then Moth taps on the den.
"Can I come in?" she says.
"Have you got six legs?" says Bob.
"Yes, I have. I am an insect,"
says Moth.

Tap, tap, tap!

Moth brings some nuts. Bob and
Ant and Moth sit in the den
and crunch the nuts.

Then Toad taps on the den.
"Can I be in the club?" he says.

"Are you an insect, Toad?" says Bob.
"No, he's not!" says Ant.
"Toads like to EAT insects,"
says Moth.

"Then you can't come in,"
Bob tells Toad.

Cockroach taps on Bob's den.
He brings a drink and ten buns.
"Yum yum," says Bob. They eat
the buns and sip the drink.

Then Mum Bug yells, "Bob!
Come in!"

Mum gives Bob some roast chicken.

"Eat up, Bob," she says.

"I'm not hungry," says Bob.

Songbirds

Where is the Snail?

Story by Julia Donaldson
Pictures by Kay Widdowson
Series editor Clare Kirtley

OXFORD
UNIVERSITY PRESS

Tips for reading Where is the Snail? together

This book practises this letter pattern:

ai

Ask your child to point to this letter pattern and say the sound (*ai* as in *snail*). Look out for this letter pattern in the story.

Your child might find these words tricky:

**the   flamingo   one   you   after
her   are   octopus   how   many**

These words are common, but your child may not be able to sound them out yet. Say the words for your child if they do not know them.

Before you begin, ask your child to read the title. Remind your child to read words they do not recognise by sounding out and blending. Look at the picture together. What do you think this story is about?

Remind your child to read unfamiliar words by saying the individual sounds separately and then blending them together quickly to read the word. When you have finished reading the story, look through it again and:

- Ask your child, *Which animals are awake at night?* (The bat and the fox.)

- Find and read two words on pages 72 and 73 which rhyme (*tail, snail*). Point to the letter pattern that makes the long vowel sound in each word. Say what sound this letter pattern makes (*ai*). Find and read some more words in the book which contain the letter pattern *ai* (*sails, wait*).

A red parrot flaps its wings.
A chimp swings.
A pink flamingo stands on one leg.
But can you see the snail?

Hens cluck.
Ducks quack.

A black cat sits in the sun.
But can you see the snail?

A squirrel cracks a nut.
A thrush sings in its nest.

A web hangs from a twig.
But can you see the snail?

A boat sails.
A gull pecks at a sandwich.

A crab runs across a rock.
But can you see the snail?

A frog jumps.
A duck swims across the pond.

Seven ducklings swim after her.
But can you see the snail?

Bees buzz.
A man digs.

A robin sits on a twig.
But can you see the snail?

69

Bats flit.
A fox hunts.

In the street, the lamps are lit.
But can you see the snail?

A cat licks her kittens.
A dog wags his tail.

A rabbit munches a carrot.
But can you see the snail?

Six pink fish swim along.
A big black fish snaps at them.
An octopus lies in wait.
How many snails can you see?

Songbirds

Stop Chatting, Bill

Story by Julia Donaldson

Pictures by Ross Collins

Series editor Clare Kirtley

OXFORD
UNIVERSITY PRESS

Tips for reading Stop Chatting, Bill together

This book practises this letter pattern:

oo

Ask your child to point to this letter pattern and say the sound (*oo* as in *too*). Look out for this letter pattern in the story.

Your child might find these words tricky:

the to of go come says what you school she he like my said

These words are common, but your child may not be able to sound them out yet. Say the words for your child if they do not know them.

Before you begin, ask your child to read the title. Remind your child to read words they do not recognise by sounding out and blending. Look at the picture together. What do you think this story is about?

Remind your child to read unfamiliar words by saying the individual sounds separately and then blending them together quickly to read the word. When you have finished reading the story, look through it again and:

- Ask your child, *Why didn't Bill tell everyone about his tooth?* (Miss Hill had told him to stop chatting.)

- Point to the letter pattern that makes the long vowel sound in *smooth*. Say what sound this letter pattern makes (*oo* as in *moon*). Find and read some more words in the book which contain the letter pattern *oo* (*school, too, tooth*).

"Come and sit on the mat," says Miss Hill.

"What did you bring to school, Flick?" says Miss Hill.
Flick has a magnet. "It can pick up pins," she says.

The pins stick to the magnet. The magnet picks up lots of clips too. The children clap.

But Bill is not clapping. He is chatting to Fred.

"Stop chatting to Fred," says
Miss Hill.
"Go and sit next to Jess."

"What did you bring to school, Fred?" says Miss Hill.
Fred has a box of shells.

"I like this smooth pink shell best," he says. The children clap.

But Bill is not clapping. He is chatting to Jess.

"Stop chatting to Jess," says Miss Hill. "Go and sit next to the fish tank."

"What did you bring in, Jess?" says Miss Hill.

"This is my pet stick insect," says Jess. "It can lift its left leg."

The stick insect lifts its leg.
The children clap.

But Bill is not clapping. He is chatting to the fish!

"Stop chatting to the fish, Bill," says Miss Hill. "What did you bring in?"

Bill stands up. He has a tooth in his hand.
"Well?" says Miss Hill.
But Bill just stands still.

"Go on," says Miss Hill. "Tell us about the tooth."

"But Miss," says Bill. "You said I had to stop chatting."

Songbirds

Back to Bed

Story by Julia Donaldson
Pictures by Joelle Dreidemy
Series editor Clare Kirtley

OXFORD
UNIVERSITY PRESS

Tips for reading Back to Bed together

This book practises this letter pattern:

oo

Ask your child to point to this letter pattern and say the sound (*oo* as in *book*). Look out for this letter pattern in the story.

Your child might find these words tricky:

go going to of the are after they says have read reading one she my out you her he gives come comes was were

These words are common, but your child may not be able to sound them out yet. Say the words for your child if they do not know them.

Before you begin, ask your child to read the title. Remind your child to read words they do not recognise by sounding out and blending. Look at the picture together. What do you think this story is about?

When you have finished reading the story, look through it again and:

- Ask your child, *Why did Liz yell at Beth and Alex?* (She was annoyed because they would not go back to bed.)
- Find and read two words on pages 95 and 96 which rhyme (*look, book*). Point to the letter pattern that makes the vowel sound in these words. Say what sound this letter pattern makes (*oo* as in *good*). Think of other words which rhyme with *look* (e.g. *cook, hook, crook, took, shook*). Try and write some on a piece of paper.

Mum and Dad are going to see a film. Liz comes to look after Beth and Alex. "They must go to bed at seven," says Mum.

Beth and Alex have wooden bunk
beds. Liz tucks them up.
"Read us a book!" says Alex.

Liz ends up reading six books.

"Sing us a song!" says Beth.

"Just one song," says Liz. But she ends up singing six songs.

Liz is having a cup of coffee. In comes Beth.
"My doll fell out of bed," she says.
"Will you kiss her foot?"

Liz kisses the doll's foot. Then,
"Back to bed," she says.

Liz has a sip of coffee. In comes
Alex. He has hiccups.

Liz gives Alex a drink. Then,
"Back to bed," she says.

In comes Beth. "Alex is jumping on the bed," she says.

"Back to bed, Alex," says Liz.

Alex comes in. "Beth has got Mum's lipstick," he says.

"BACK TO BED!" Liz yells.

Mum and Dad come back.
"Was the film good?" says Liz.

"Yes," says Dad. "And were Beth and Alex good?"

"Yes!" says Liz.